Moments of Matrescence

Hannah Campbell

BookLeaf Publishing

Presentation by *BookLeaf Publishing*

Web: www.bookleafpub.com

E-mail: info@bookleafpub.com

ISBN: 9789357741132

First edition 2023

*For my beautiful babies, who brought me
back home to myself.*

ACKNOWLEDGEMENT

Sharing a deep gratitude for my parents, my husband, my friends and my children - all of whom inspire me every day.

PREFACE

Working as a coach, doula and hypnobirthing teacher gives me a great sense of purpose and satisfaction in life.

Doing this work, alongside my own experiences of motherhood and miscarriage, has opened my eyes to the narratives we are told. Far too many of us enter into this transitional period of our lives with a preconceived idea of who we should be and what we should do.

Moments of Matrescence is one woman's exploration of what it means to be a mother, what it means to have power and purpose as a mother, and how to find a new narrative in the chaos of it all.

A season

Red hair and sticky hands,
Cupping his soft cheeks.
Sneaky smiles and a belly laugh
A joke only the two of you know.

Me, an island, holding demands,
Losing tracks of the hours and weeks.
Scalding the end of the day into a hot bath,
Still learning the art of going with the flow.

The dead of night, your cries so loud,
You yearn for me, arms outstretched.
My instincts have my mind cowed,
Tiredness hangs, on my face etched.

My chest, your home, your safest space,
Your soft breath calming is my reason.
Knowing deep down this is the place,
And it really is just all a season.

At least

At least they say

At least it was early
At least you have one
At least there is next time
At least it's not further along
At least it was quick
At least you still can
At least you're at home
At least you're not sick

At least, at least, at least
Yet my heart screams out

I counted down months for that blue line
One small hand doesn't help at the time
Trying again sounds like pain and sorrow
It doesn't matter someone else is tomorrow
Next time I'll be full of worry and fears
I don't feel at home though all of my tears
Heartbreak is sickness, and it cuts deep
The nights are so long without any sleep

So perhaps not at least and instead

I am here and I hear you
I see your pain
We don't need to worry about 'again'
Instead let's just wait
Feel it and make space
And deal with this shit you've got on your plate.

Cord

It pulses away all curly and blue
This cord that keeps me connected to you

A lifeline, a channel, a glorious line
That keeps your body connected to mine

A constant flow of love, food and blood
Body doing just as it should

I watch what I do, never alone
You stay nestled in that safe home

When it is time for you to come out
We wait for the almighty big shout

Instead you move slowly, not yet a cry
The midwives they panic, not willing to try

Wait for our bodies to do their magic,
They don't see it which feels so tragic

My skin on yours, your face near my breast
Our heartbeats in sync as you just rest

I know you just need a few seconds more
Like your big brother did before

But in they come with their scissors

And sever

Us

Apart

She

She sits behind the flash capturing
Those small laughs and smiles
She finds an endless capacity for
Reaching and rocking and shushing

She remembers the nights they arrived
The way her body opened slowly like a rose
She loved the way her breath became power,
Deeper and roaring and strong

She knows the power in stillness watching
Those small souls discover the world
She remembers when she did it herself
Adventure and exploring and wonder

She loves endlessly, a never-ending pot
Of cuddles and kisses and tickles
She feels so intensely, and always
loving and caring and intense

New narrative

We are sold a story of fear and of pain
Of never wanting to do it again
Of screaming, of crying, or wailing too
Of hands squeezed too tight, turning blue

Instead it was power, perfect and pure
Instead it was easing and hearing me roar
Instead it was primal, and beautiful too
My body that rocked and breath that blew

A body that rolled, writhed with charm
A body that opened with comfort and calm
A body that held you as you gently
Slipped into hands with wide eyes aplenty

Why don't they say how primal it is
Why don't they say how hormones fizz
Why don't they say how amazing it feels
As our body and baby work like cog wheels

A narrative that is old and is tired
A narrative that is badly wired
A narrative that is as loud as a train
We are sold a story of fear and of pain

But oh
How I'd do it again, again, again

This is the place

Nana, he cries
This is the place!
As I watch smiles
Creep over your face.

Your arms open wide
You cuddle him tight
The love is tangible
As he says with might

This is my Nana,
This is the place!
As I see his excitement
Take over his face.

He marches inside
Barefoot aplenty.
Oh there is Molly!
He strokes her so gently.

His laugh is so loud
It's as if he knew
Seeing you together
A bright little crew

Would make me realise this is the place
The place of wonder, of love and of grace
The place that isn't just bricks and mortar
But the place I have as your daughter

Coming home

They said I'd want you to be smaller
Or tighter
Or stronger

They said I'd feel bad with the lines
And stretches
And softness

They said I'd look frumpy
Look wobbly
Look weird

But by being your home,
I have come home

Home to softness
Home to safety
Home to confidence
Home to calm

Because there's worth in the wobbles
The lines and the grooves
New pathways foraged in my skin
On the way not only to you

But back to myself.

Rowan tree

So tiny and helpless
Covered in tubes
Nothing to do but sit
And watch you

Feeling so lost as they come
And they go
Wondering why it feels
So slow

The hours inch by at
Snails pace
No sign of improvement
The looks on their face

The loneliest hours in
Early morn
Yearning for closeness
Every dawn

So limp and so lifeless
My boy and my heart
So painful to be so close
Yet far apart

Maternal instincts fiery
Flooding
Milk surging and surging
Telling me something

So I pump and I pump
Filling the cups
Hoping you'll wake soon
To sup

Slides down your tube into
Your tummy
Shouting I'm here! I am
Your mummy

A matter of hours and your
Eyes, well they flicker
The milk goes down
Quicker and quicker

Then one day, your eyes
Curious and round
Born again, this time with
Sound

Small squeaks, oh just the best
As you root and nuzzle for
My breast

The days go on and boy you
Are strong
My ears are full of your
Song

You stretch and you reach
Your little pink tongue
Searching and searching
For mum

Now we are home
We are safe
We are free

I am home with my Rowan tree.

Career Woman

She didn't want a career
After kids arrived
Cared less or didn't want it
Or so they surmised

But how little they knew
How small minded they were
To work was a verb
And doing was her

Maybe she was tired
Of all the small digs
About leaving on time
And collecting sick kids

Maybe she was raring
And waiting to thrive
But countless red tape
And rolled senior eyes

Made her consider
What was it for
To miss her children
Leaving them at the door

Why was she letting herself
Get so small?
Why did her passion
Not matter at all?

If she wasn't going to fit the mould
If she was honest and open and true
Then they'd headbutt with a look that
Said we don't want you

When the people around her
Cared so little, so less
Why was she struggling
And trying to impress?

Yes maybe beers
And jokes after hours
Didn't suit these days
Instead, her powers

Lay in drive, in determination,
In empathy and keen
Yet somehow not quite
Perceived as part of the team

So she left it and moved on
To a different career
One where she'd lead
She would always cheer

For herself and her drive
Her empathy and keen
Loving life on her very own team.

The rainbow

The very first sight of that bright magenta
I walked into work, trying to pretend
Just spotting I said
Maybe

Everything is fine, I'm meant to be here
What would they think
If I scurried away
And all was fine the very next day?

The universe intervened
Covid. Isolation please!

So we bundled and burrowed,
Our brows firm with furrows
Feeling indigo blue

Uncertain. Not sure.
Is this really it?

Ten weeks of bliss
Disappearing like that?

Each day getting worse
As my body would rock

And squeeze and hurt
Both inside and out

Work start to peck
What's going on?
Are you working or not
I hope it's not long

Don't leave the shit jobs
Down to me
What do you want
You tell us

If only they'd said no work
Until you're ready
And even then
We'll take it steady

Ten days of prison
Can't scan to find out
Then on the last day
As I crawl and crept

To that cosy room where we slept
A rainbow
Filled out the room from wall to wall
And I know you said bye. Sorry for it all.

Sat dealing with the knowing
You really were gone
But grateful and amazed that
You left me a song

In the colours that beamed
From wall to wall
The shades that said
You handled it all

In the instinct it passed me
We're worth more than this
Put yourself first

So the very next day
When the sonographer said
Your uterus isn't pregnant

(Your baby is dead)

I lay in the dark, all alone of course
Peeled my pants back on
Wiped away tears

Strode into the cold fresh air
Numb with the news I had to share

The very next day, back on the grind
Not time to recover, not for my kind

Greeted by words cold and unfeeling
At least it was only early
There's away next time
As I sat in the bathroom
Cry, cry, cry

Ships

Nothing said between the hours
Of twelve and six count
Is the rule

Let's face it neither of us really
Knows what we are saying
When we duel

Some nights we sneak touch
It's not always so easy
Yet we do

We yearn for each other
In unexpected ways
Just us two

A back stroke or bum tap
A familiar hand on
My warm skin

Good old days they were now
it is different but
The same still

Ships passing in the night

A blur of sleep and rage
Looks could kill

Yet the sunrises a new day
And it is all forgotten with
A head kiss

Hot tea and toast burning
Tired faces smiling familiar
I still miss

Your smell, my favourite place
In the morning I get to sneak
A small bit

The days feel long yet the weeks
Rush by in a flash and we say
We did it

Suddenly three, sleeping through
Now what to do when we wake
Early morning

We can sink and settle deep
Back into our foundations and
Remember

This house

She stands tall, wide like a river
So much of us packed into her
Her arms embrace us all, her soft eye
watches over us as we potter

The walls are patchy, small swipes
From tiny hands, remnants flicked
During animated dinner times
A masterpiece of mealtime chaos

Rooms half done, we tried new things
And decided we liked it the old way better
The floorboards creak sometimes, She
Bends and flexes with the weight of us.

Each space within her tells our story
The room we heard our first babe cry
Walls that have felt the heat of our rage
The door that drops open like a yawn

Her security is unspoken but known
The way she holds our souls in bricks
A haven for our hearts and minds
And steps which our children tread.

He Will

The weight of raising him
Weighs heavy on me

A man who opens his heart freely
Yet knows who can hold space

A man who speaks his mind with ease
Yet doesn't silence those who can't

A man who is tender and caring
Yet does not bend to any whim

A man who makes others feel safe
Yet doesn't sacrifice his own

A man who leaps with faith for himself
Yet is not blind to his society

A man who loves deeply and raw
Yet does not give to everyone

A man who is respectful and just
Yet holds respect for himself also

A man who leans into opportunity

Yet doesn't trample on others

A man who can make sense of the
Ever evolving guidelines of
What it means to be a man

One thing is certain is that he will
Always be my little boy

Little Red Fox

Conker hair and a sun flecked face
Small paws which clasp at mine
A button nose, often crinkled
Dainty limbs which curl in

A sunshine smile, small white teeth
A raucous snore as you sleep
Tiny curved nails, pink like shells
Expressive eyebrows often furrowed

A love to climb, an urge to explore
A great big breath once outdoors
The marionette run, all limbs akimbo
Wild and as free as the wind

Fearless adventure, explorer filling
the air with marvellous sound

We settle down under the blanket
You say 'tuck me in mummy!'
Deep breaths of your smell
Settle my heart and soul

How lucky am I to have you
Little red fox.

Is it enough?

Is it enough that every second thought is of you,
That I find smiles when I feel blue?
Is it enough I lend my body for your rest,
That I always try my best?

Is it enough that I forget to eat
That I find people to meet?
Is it enough I don't always play,
That I sometimes wonder what to say?

Is it enough that I sometimes shout,
That I forget to care it out?
Is it enough that I give you choices,
That I try give you a voice?

Is it enough that I feel the guilt,
That I softly tuck your quilt?
Is it enough that I gently get you dressed,
That I always try my best?

Returning

My body is a map,
Of the journey we have travelled
A few new lines and softness,
Stretched and stronger.

Your body has changed,
I trace the paths we've walked
On your back and kind face,
Tired and tender.

My mind feels worn,
From sleepless nights and guiding
Our small humans to safety,
Secure and safer.

Your mind is distant,
From work and life overwhelm
Taking day one step at a time,
Caring and calmer.

We meet at odd times,
Stolen seconds whilst they sleep
Soundly in their beds,
Safe and snoring.

Too much time has passed
Since our last meeting
I am losing track of the days,
Yearning and yearning.

We know what to do like
Jigsaw pieces or places on
A map that intertwine,
Returning, returning, returning.

Letting Go

We learnt how to breathe, in the very first class
We didn't know we'd been doing it wrong.
We learnt how to calm our minds, to learn anew,
We didn't know how much we'd taken on.

We learnt how to release and relax, something
new
We didn't know how much tension we held.
We learnt how to move and stretch into things,
We didn't realise our bones were so tired.

We learnt how to trust our intuition, to listen
We didn't know how distant we were
We learnt how to trust our gut and listen
We didn't realise how deaf we had become.

We learnt the art of letting go,
Of breathing and listening
Of releasing expectation, assumption and more
We didn't realise how wrong we had it before.

Darkness

The nights feel so long, your milky breath
Falls against my cold cheek
The world sits in silence and I wonder
How many others sit like me

Your tiny hands knead me like bread
I feel so stretched and paper thin
At times I wonder how I manage
With so little to fill my tank

Your heart sits alongside mine,
That familiar beat murmuring
My body hears it and sighs deeply
I can do this, just one more night

How is it so that as the darkness fills the room
I feel like you are back there, deep in my womb